'There was a robbery near Portsmouth at three o'clock this afternoon. Some men put a tree on the road and stopped a security van. They took half a million pounds.'

Half a million pounds is on the road to London. But it will never get there. Petra, Harry, George and Andy are waiting, and they're going to take the money with them. And nobody's going to stop them. *Nobody.*

But, then, they don't know Mark and Zoe, the children on the farm fifty kilometres away. When they stop at the farm, they will meet them – and Topaz the horse too!

John Escott was born in a small town in Somerset, in the west of England. He now lives with his wife in Bournemouth, in Dorset, by the sea in the south of England.

He is the writer of many books, and many of these are detective stories. Most of them are about people living in the south and west of England. Portsmouth is a city not too far from his home. John says he sometimes thinks of the name of a book first, and then the story. This happened with *Money to Burn*.

When John is not writing, he likes walking by the sea.

To the teacher:

In addition to all the language forms of Level One, which are used again at this level of the series, the main verb forms and tenses used at Level Two are:

- common irregular forms of past simple verbs, *going to* (for prediction and to state intention) and common phrasal verbs
- modal verbs: *will* and *won't* (to express willingness) and *must* (to express obligation or necessity).

Also used are:

- adverbs: irregular adverbs of manner, further adverbs of place and time
- prepositions: of movement, further prepositions and prepositional phrases of place and time
- adjectives: comparison of similars (*as . . . as*) and of dissimilars (*-er than, the . . . -est in/of, more* and *most . . .*)
- conjunctions: *so* (consequences), *because* (reasons), *before/ after/when* (for sequencing)
- indirect speech (statements).

Specific attention is paid to vocabulary development in the Vocabulary Work exercises at the end of the book. These exercises are aimed at training students to enlarge their vocabulary systematically through intelligent reading and effective use of a dictionary.

To the student:

Dictionary Words:

- some words in this book are darker black than others. Look them up in your dictionary or try to understand them without a dictionary first, and then look them up later.

Money to Burn

JOHN ESCOTT

Level 2

Series Editor: Derek Strange

PENGUIN BOOKS

PENGUIN BOOKS

Published by the Penguin Group
Penguin Books Ltd, 27 Wrights Lane, London W8 5TZ, England
Penguin Books USA Inc., 375 Hudson Street, New York, New York 10014, USA
Penguin Books Australia Ltd, Ringwood, Victoria, Australia
Penguin Books Canada Ltd, 10 Alcorn Avenue, Toronto, Ontario, Canada M4V 3B2
Penguin Books (NZ) Ltd, 182–190 Wairau Road, Auckland 10, New Zealand

Penguin Books Ltd, Registered Offices: Harmondsworth, Middlesex, England

First published by Penguin Books 1993
1 3 5 7 9 10 8 6 4 2

Text copyright © John Escott 1993
Illustrations copyright © Kay Dixey 1993
All rights reserved

The moral right of the author and of the illustrator has been asserted

Typeset by Datix International Limited, Bungay, Suffolk
Set in 12/14pt Lasercomp Bembo
Printed in England by Clays Ltd, St Ives plc

Before you read

Look at the picture and answer the questions.

1 What time of year do you think it is? Summer or winter?

2 Which of the following things can you see in the picture?
   a *a church*   b *a car*   c *a young woman*
   d *a man wearing a hat*   e *a bus*

3 There is a tree across the small road. Can a car get by it?

4 What do you think is going to happen next?

5 Do you think this story is going to be:
  a *a sad story?*   b *an exciting story?*
  c *a story to make you laugh?*

Chapter One

ROBBERY!

It is a wet afternoon in November, and the winds are strong. On a road near the river, three men are cutting down a tree. When the tree is down, they pull it on to the road and then go to wait behind some other trees. Their red car is near them, ready to drive away quickly. It is a small, quiet road.

A hundred metres away, a woman called Petra is watching the big road from the city. She is waiting for a blue **security van**. Next to Petra, there is a **sign** across the road near the river. It says: ROAD CLOSED. The strong winds push over the sign, and Petra puts it back again.

Where's the security van? she thinks. Perhaps it's late because the **storm** is bad.

She looks along the quiet road and sees the tree, ready to stop the van. Harry and George and Andy are behind the other trees.

Nothing must go wrong, thinks Petra.

Two cars slow down, ready to turn into the road by the river. Then they see the ROAD CLOSED sign and go on.

Petra smiles. They think it's closed because of the weather, she thinks. She starts to walk up and down in the rain. Her face and hair are wet, and she is cold. Petra is not afraid, but she does not like waiting. She is twenty-five years old. Older than Andy, but not as old as Harry and George.

Suddenly, Petra hears something. She looks along the big road and sees the blue security van coming. She quickly moves the ROAD CLOSED sign away, then she runs along by the river to the other three men.

'It's coming!' she **shouts**.

Harry is smoking a cigarette and Petra sees him throw it in the river. George puts a hand in his coat and pulls out a gun.

Andy looks at his watch. 'Nearly three o'clock,' he says. 'It's late.' He looks afraid.

♦

The security van is taking money to the Bank of England. The money is old and dirty **banknotes**. They are going to be **burned**. There are two men in the security van, one of them driving.

'The storm is getting worse,' the driver says.

The other man looks at the trees **blowing** in the strong wind. 'I think you're right,' he says.

The blue van turns into the road near the river. The driver sees the tree on the road and starts to slow down.

'Do you think the wind blew that tree down, Frank?' he says.

'Yes,' says the other man. 'Stay in the van, Charlie. Perhaps I can move it.'

He opens the door and jumps down from the van. Then he walks across to the tree and tries to push it off the road.

'It's too heavy!' he shouts.

Three men run out from behind the trees by the road. They are carrying guns.

Charlie opens his door and comes to help.

Three men run out from behind the trees by the road. They are carrying guns.

◆

Fifty kilometres away, a girl and a boy are coming home from school on their bikes. The girl is fourteen years old and her name is Zoe Harper. The boy is her brother, and his name is Mark. He is twelve.

They are going along a small road between two lines of trees. It is difficult trying to stay on the bikes in the strong wind.

'I don't like storms,' shouts Zoe.

Mark does not hear her. All he hears is the wind. The two children live on a **farm**, two kilometres from their school. Usually it does not take very long to get home, but the storm is making them late. It is half past three.

They turn a corner and see the farm. A light is on in the farm house. Zoe sees her mother by the kitchen window but her father is outside. He is trying to put up a **fence**, but the wind is blowing it down again.

'Let's help Dad,' says Zoe, getting off her bike.

They put their bikes inside the old **barn**. When they come out again, they see a tree begin to come down near the fence.

'Dad!' shouts Zoe. 'Look out!'

She sees her father start to move away, but he is too late. The tree comes down on him.

Zoe runs across from the barn. She hears her mother come out of the house shouting, 'Ted! Ted!' Mark is running now.

*Zoe sees her father start to move away, but he is too late.
The tree comes down on him.*

Mr Harper tries to push the tree away, and his wife and children help him. There is **blood** on his face.

'My arm – !' he shouts when they pull the tree off him.

'Did the tree break your arm?' says Mrs Harper.

'Yes, I – I think it did,' says her husband.

They help him walk to the house and they all go into the kitchen.

'You must go to the hospital, Ted,' says Mrs Harper. She washes the blood off his face. 'I can drive you.'

'OK,' says Mr Harper. He looks out of the window. 'Driving is dangerous in this weather.'

'The children can stay here,' says Mrs Harper. 'Jean is coming soon.'

Jean Fisher is a friend. She is coming to stay with the Harper family.

'Yes, we can stay here,' says Zoe. 'We're not afraid.'

Mark looks at her. He *is* afraid, thinks Zoe, but he's not telling Mum.

Chapter Two

HALF A MILLION POUNDS!

The rain is heavy and it is difficult to see along the road. The red car moves slowly. The three men are inside, the woman is driving. She is trying to see through the rain.

'Can't you go faster?' says George. He is sitting in the front next to Petra.

'No, I can't,' says Petra. 'The rain's getting worse every minute.'

The woman is driving. She is trying to see through the rain.

'We have to get to London,' says George.

'I don't like this,' says Petra. 'There's a lot of water on the road. It's difficult to drive.'

'Perhaps it's better on the smaller roads,' says Andy from the back seat.

Petra turns off the big road, but there is more water on the smaller road. 'It's **flooded**,' she says. The car moves very slowly through the water. 'We must find a place to stop.'

The men say nothing for a minute, then Harry says, 'Yeah, Petra's right. We can't get to London today.'

'Where can we stop?' asks George.

'I don't know,' says Petra.

George looks at his watch, then puts the car radio on.

'. . . and he's coming from America, next week.' says a woman on the radio. 'There was a robbery near Portsmouth at three o'clock this afternoon. Some men put a tree on the road and stopped a security van. They took half a million pounds in banknotes – old and dirty banknotes to be burned at the Bank of England. The police are looking for three men and a woman in a red car. They have guns and are dangerous.

'The weather is getting worse. Many roads are flooded, and police are asking drivers to stay at home . . .'

'Half a million pounds!' says Andy. 'We're rich!'

'Yeah, and all old banknotes,' says Harry. He is thinking about the four large black bags in the back of the car. 'I always liked old things,' he says, laughing.

'The police know the colour of this car,' says George. 'We're going to have to get a different one.'

'And we're going to have to find a place to stop,' says Petra. 'Driving is dangerous in this weather.'

'Where are we?' asks Andy.

'I don't know,' says Petra. She is tired.

◆

At the farm, Zoe hears the phone. She goes to answer it. 'Hallo?' she says.

'Is that Zoe?' says the woman on the phone. 'This is Jean Fisher. Can I speak to your Mum?'

'Mum's at the hospital with Dad,' says Zoe. 'Dad had an accident.'

'What happened?' asks Jean Fisher.

Zoe tells her about the tree and her Dad's arm. 'They're coming back later,' she says. 'Are you coming soon?'

'No,' says Jean Fisher. 'I phoned to tell you. The weather is bad and the roads are flooded. I can't get to the farm today.'

Zoe is looking at Mark. He is watching her speak into the phone. What am I going to tell him? she thinks. When he hears that Jean Fisher can't come, he's going to be afraid.

'When are you coming?' she asks Jean Fisher.

'Tomorrow,' says the woman. 'When the weather is better.'

'OK, see you then,' says Zoe. She puts down the phone.

'Who was that?' asks Mark.

'Jean Fisher,' says Zoe.

'Is she coming soon?' he asks.

'She's going to be a little late,' says Zoe.

Chapter Three

THE ROBBERS ARRIVE

'Look over there, a kilometre or two across the **fields**,' says George. 'A house!'

Petra and the others look across the flooded fields. It is nearly half past four and the afternoon is getting darker. Petra sees a light in a window. 'It's a farm house,' she says. 'There's a light. Somebody's there.'

'That's OK,' laughs Andy. 'They're going to be pleased to see us.'

'Yeah,' says Harry. 'And perhaps they've got some food. I'm hungry.'

'We're all hungry,' says George. 'We can have something to eat and stay there tonight.'

Petra turns the car into the next road and goes down to the farm.

◆

Zoe and Mark are watching the TV. A man is talking about a robbery from a security van.

'Half a million pounds!' says Mark. 'That's a lot of money. And all of it old banknotes, to be burned. How exciting!'

'It happened near Portsmouth,' says Zoe. 'That's not far from here. Where are the robbers now?'

'Perhaps they're going to London,' says Mark. 'It only takes two hours by car.'

The weather's bad, thinks Zoe. Perhaps they can't get to London in this storm. But she does not want Mark to be afraid, so she says nothing.

Petra and the others look across the flooded fields . . . 'It's a farm house,' she says.

Mark goes to the window and looks out. 'Do you think the **horses** are OK?' he says. 'Brownie doesn't like storms.'

'I forgot all about them!' says Zoe. 'After Dad's accident, I forgot to go and see Topaz. Let's go and look now.'

Topaz is Zoe's horse. She likes to go across the fields and along the roads near the farm on him. Mark has a smaller horse called Brownie.

They put on their coats and go outside. The wind is not so strong now and it is not raining so hard. The two of them run across to the **stables**, looking at the flooded fields.

Did Mum and Dad get to the hospital OK? thinks Zoe.

There are three horses in the stables: Topaz, Brownie, and a big white horse called Mercury. Mercury is Zoe's father's horse.

'Hallo, Topaz,' says Zoe. 'I'm sorry I forgot about you.' She pulls his ear because she knows he likes her to do this. Then she puts an arm round him and the horse moves closer to her.

'Is Brownie OK?' she asks Mark.

'Yes,' says Mark.

'Let's have a look at Mercury,' says Zoe.

The big white horse is pleased to see Zoe and moves across to her. Suddenly, the animal stops and turns its head to the door.

'What is it, Mercury?' says Zoe. 'Did you hear something?' She listens and hears the sound of a car.

'Mum and Dad are back!' says Mark, running across to the door of the stables. 'That was quick.'

Zoe and Mark run across to the stables, looking at the flooded fields.

'Perhaps they didn't get through the flooded roads,' says Zoe, following him. 'Perhaps they didn't get to the hospital.' She sees the car coming down the road to the farm. 'That's not Dad's car.'

'Perhaps it's Jean Fisher,' says Mark.

'No, it's not,' says Zoe. Suddenly, she is afraid. 'Go back into the stables,' she tells Mark, pushing him in front of her.

'What's wrong?' asks Mark. Now he is looking afraid.

'I – I don't know,' says Zoe.

She watches the car get closer to the farm house. It is red. It stops near the house and three men and a woman get out.

'What did the man on TV say earlier?' says Zoe. 'A red car?'

'Yes, it was red. And three men and a woman were in it,' says Mark, looking afraid. 'They – they're the robbers! What are we going to do?'

Chapter Four

HARRY AND THE HORSES

George looks at the farm house, then at the buildings near it. 'There's a barn over there,' he tells Petra. 'Go and see if you can get the car in it. We don't want this car to be seen.'

'Who can see it here?' says Harry.

'The police are looking for us, remember?' says Andy.

'And they have helicopters,' says George.

'. . . three men and a woman,' says Mark, looking afraid.
'They – they're the robbers! What are we going to do?'

Petra opens the barn doors and looks inside. 'There's nothing in here now, but a car was here,' she shouts to the others. 'Perhaps everybody is out.'

'There are lights on in the house,' says Andy.

'Let's go and see,' says George.

Petra drives the car into the old barn and the three men go over to the house. George takes his gun from his coat. Harry does the same and goes to the front door. George and Andy go to the back door. They look through the windows but can see nobody in the kitchen.

'It's all very quiet,' says Andy.

George opens the back door and goes inside. 'Is anybody here?' he shouts.

'Look!' says Andy. He sees some blood on the floor. 'Somebody had an accident.'

George goes to look. 'Perhaps they've gone to the hospital,' he says. 'Perhaps they had to leave quickly. Go and let Harry in through the front door.'

Andy goes through to the front of the house and Petra comes in the back door.

'I've put the car in the barn and shut the doors,' she says. 'There's no other car here.'

'Nobody's here,' says George. 'We think they've gone to the hospital.' He shows Petra the blood. 'Somebody had an accident.'

'There's a tree down over near the fence,' Petra tells him. 'Perhaps somebody was under it.'

Harry comes from the front of the house. 'Andy's gone to look in the other rooms,' he says.

'There's nobody in the barn, but there are stables outside,' says Petra.

'Go and look round them, Harry,' says George.

'Look!' says Andy. He sees some blood on the floor.
'Somebody had an accident.'

'I don't like horses,' says Harry.

'Do it!' George tells him.

'OK,' says Harry, and he goes out of the back door.

'What about the money?' asks Petra.

'It can stay in the car,' says George. 'We can get it after we've had something to eat. Let's find some food.'

The two of them start opening cupboards.

♦

Mark is watching from the doors of the stables. He sees Harry come out of the house.

'Somebody's coming!' he says, moving back from the door. 'It's one of the men.'

'I can see him,' says Zoe quietly, looking over his head. The horses have heard somebody coming, too. They are moving around and making sounds. Zoe goes over to them, Mark following her.

'Be quiet!' Zoe tells Topaz, but the horse doesn't listen to her.

'What can we do?' Mark says. 'The man is going to find us.'

Zoe thinks for a minute, then she says, 'Get down on the floor, Topaz.' She hits him on the back, and the horse sits down on the floor of the stables. 'Get down on the floor behind Topaz,' she tells Mark. 'Quickly!'

Marks sits down on the floor and Zoe gets down next to him. 'Don't move,' Zoe tells her brother. 'They can't see us from the door.' She puts a hand on her horse. 'And please don't get up, Topaz. We don't want the man to find us in here.'

A minute later, Harry comes into the stables. Topaz gives a little jump but he doesn't stand up. Harry is afraid. He doesn't like animals, and he doesn't like to be near horses. He's afraid of them. He lights a cigarette with his **lighter** and looks round the stables, standing near the door.

'I'm not going in there,' he says quietly. 'There's nobody in the place, only horses. I can see that from here.'

The big white horse comes across to him. Harry moves away quickly. 'Get back!' he tells the horse. 'Go away!' The horse is getting closer and closer. Harry quickly shuts the door of the stables and runs back to the house.

Chapter Five

THE HELICOPTER

When everything is quiet again, Mark and Zoe get up from the floor. 'It's lucky he doesn't like horses,' says Zoe.

'What can we do now?' asks Mark.

'We must get the police,' says his sister.

'But the phone is in the house,' says Mark. 'We can't use it.'

'We must do *something*!' says Zoe. 'Where did they put the car? In the barn?'

'Yes,' says Mark. 'Why?'

'Perhaps there's a phone in the car,' says Zoe.

'Perhaps there is!' says Mark. 'Let's go and see.'

'No, you stay here,' says Zoe. 'I can go. I don't want them to catch me *and* you.'

'OK,' says Mark. 'But be careful.'

Zoe looks round the door of the stables and sees Harry going back inside the house. She sees the men and the woman in the kitchen. They are taking food from the cupboards and putting it on the table. Zoe is angry. That's our food they're taking! she thinks.

She is going out of the door when she puts her foot on something. Something small and hard on the floor. Zoe looks down.

It is a lighter . . . but her father and mother don't smoke.

That man used it to light a cigarette, she thinks. It's dangerous to light cigarettes in stables. It can start a fire. She picks up the lighter and puts it in her jeans.

Zoe moves carefully along the outside of the stables. She looks across to the house, but nobody is looking out of the window. Moving quickly and quietly, Zoe runs to the barn. The barn doors are shut but she opens one and goes inside, then she shuts it again.

The red car is standing in the centre of the floor. Zoe opens the driver's door and sits in the front. She looks for a phone but there isn't one.

Perhaps I can drive the car, she thinks. I can get Mark, and we can drive into the town and get the police. I've seen Dad and Mum drive, I know I can do it.

But there is no key to start the car.

Then Zoe hears somebody talking outside. She gets out of the car and goes to the barn door, opening it a little. She looks out and sees the woman and one of the men walking across to the stables.

'George is angry with you,' the woman is saying. 'When he tells us to do something, he likes us to do it, Harry.'

Zoe looks down. It is a lighter. She picks up the lighter and puts it in her jeans.

'Yeah? OK, *you* look round the stables,' the man says. 'I'm not going inside with those horses.'

The woman laughs. 'I didn't know you were afraid of animals,' she says.

'Only horses,' says the man. He doesn't like the woman laughing at him. 'And you can look for my lighter,' he tells her. 'I think I lost it in the stables.'

'Anything you say, Harry,' the woman says, laughing again.

Zoe watches the woman go into the stables, and the man walking up and down outside. Some minutes later, she hears somebody shout. The shout comes from inside the stables.

It's Mark! thinks Zoe.

The woman comes out, pulling Mark behind her. 'I didn't find your lighter,' she tells the man, 'but I found this boy.' She turns to Mark. 'Are there any other children here?'

'N-no,' says Mark. 'Only me.'

'Where are your mother and father?' asks Harry.

'They're at the hospital,' says Mark. 'But they're coming back soon.'

'No, not soon,' says the woman, smiling. It's not a nice smile. 'The roads are flooded.'

'Let's get him into the house,' says Harry.

They push Mark over to the back door of the farm house.

'Who's this?' asks George when Petra and Harry come in with the boy.

'We found him in the stables,' says Petra.

'What's your name, boy?' asks George.

'Mark,' says Mark. He looks round the room. Are they going to kill me? he thinks.

'Who's this?' asks George when Petra and Harry come in
with the boy.

'We thought you all went to the hospital,' says Andy.

'Only Mum and Dad went,' says Mark.

'Is that right?' says Andy. He comes close and pulls Mark over to him. 'Where's your sister?'

'S-sister?' says Mark. 'I haven't got a sister.'

Andy hits him across the face. 'Yes, you have! There are two bedrooms, and one is full of girls' things.'

'She – she's away,' says Mark.

'So you *have* got a sister,' says Harry.

Mark doesn't say anything. He doesn't want them to find Zoe. Did she find a phone in the car? he thinks. Are the police coming?

'Look round the place again,' George tells Petra and the two men. 'Leave the boy with me. And bring the money in here.'

'I'll get it,' says Harry. He doesn't want to go back to the stables and the horses.

'I'll look round the other rooms again,' says Andy.

'Be quick,' George tells them.

♦

Zoe can see Mark in the kitchen with the men and the woman. Are they going to make Mark tell them about me? she thinks. Where can I go? I don't want them to find me. She looks round the barn. Then she looks up at the **roof**.

There is another floor a few metres below the roof. A **ladder** goes up to a small door, and the door opens on to it. Sometimes Zoe goes up there when she wants to read a book or to be in a quiet place.

Zoe goes up the ladder now. She moves quickly. She can hear somebody coming over to the barn. When she

Zoe goes up the ladder now. She moves quickly. She can hear somebody coming over to the barn.

is on the floor above, Zoe looks down and sees the barn door open.

Harry comes into the barn and looks round. He doesn't look up at the roof. Then he goes to the car and opens the back door. He starts to take out one of the large black bags, but he hears a sound and stops. 'What's that?' Harry says.

Zoe can hear the sound, too. There is a small window in the roof of the barn and she can see the sky above. And she can see something moving in the sky, too.

It's a **helicopter!** she thinks. Perhaps the people in the helicopter are looking at the trees the storm has blown down. Perhaps they're looking to see if they can help any car drivers or other people in flooded houses.

Harry waits in the barn. When the sound of the helicopter dies away, he leaves the black bags near the car and runs across to the house.

Petra is running from the stables. 'That was the police!' she shouts to Harry.

Zoe hears her. The police! she thinks, looking through the window in the roof of the barn. How can I let them know I'm here? What can I do?

Chapter Six

FIRE!

Petra and Harry run into the house. They all stand without moving, listening to the helicopter flying over the house again. Harry looks out of the window at it. The word POLICE is on the helicopter.

'They're looking for us, George,' says Harry. 'The woman on the radio said they were.'

'Get away from the window!' says George.

'Do you think they saw the car?' asks Andy.

'It's in the barn, remember?' says Petra. 'The police can't see through doors!'

'Where's the money?' asks George.

'In the barn,' says Harry.

'Why didn't you bring it in here?' says George, angrily.

'I – I heard the helicopter and was afraid,' says Harry. His face goes white and he quickly moves away from the window. 'They're looking for us, George, I know they are!'

'The police don't know we're here,' Petra tells him. 'All they can see is a farm house, and it's already quite dark.'

'I don't like it,' says Harry. 'Why don't we get away from here? The weather is better now. The roads –'

'We stay here!' George tells him. 'The police know the colour of that car. We have to get another.'

'When the boy's mother and father come back from the hospital, we can take their car,' says Andy.

'Yeah, that's right,' says George.

'But tonight we're staying here,' says Petra. 'I'm not driving to London tonight. Perhaps the roads are better, but I'm tired.'

'We're all tired,' says George.

◆

Zoe is coming quietly down the ladder in the barn. The police are in the helicopter, but they don't know those robbers are here, she thinks. I must tell them. I must make them see that something is wrong. How can I do that?

She walks across the barn to the door. Carefully, she looks out. She can see the kitchen window, and the woman and the three men inside the house. She can see Mark sitting on a chair by the table. He's afraid, she thinks. She looks up at the sky. Is the helicopter coming back again soon? What can I do? I know! I can start a fire so that they can see something is wrong! What can I burn? Everything is wet after the storm.

Zoe looks round the barn and sees the black bags near the back of the car. She opens one and finds it is full of old and dirty banknotes.

The money from the robbery! thinks Zoe. She takes some of the money from the bag and looks at it. The man on the TV said the Bank of England burns old banknotes. She smiles. So why don't *I* burn them?

Working quickly, Zoe pulls two of the black bags out of the door and round to the back of the barn. Then she goes back for the other two. Suddenly, she hears something and looks up at the sky.

The helicopter is coming back! she thinks. She can hear the sound getting nearer and nearer.

Quickly, Zoe takes Harry's lighter from her jeans . . .

◆

'The helicopter is coming back!' says Andy, in the kitchen.

'They can't see us, they're too far away,' George tells him.

Suddenly, Harry shouts, 'Something's burning! Look! There's smoke coming from the back of the barn!'

Zoe opens a bag and finds it is full of old and dirty banknotes.

Everybody looks out of the window and sees the light and smoke from the fire.

'Stay with the boy!' George tells Petra.

The three men run out of the house and round to the back of the barn. Harry sees the black bags. 'Somebody's burning our money!' he shouts.

The banknotes are burning well, smoke going up into the sky. George and Harry run across to the burning banknotes, but the fire is too hot and they have to get back again.

Nobody sees Zoe running to the house. Her face is hot from the fire. She pushes open the back door.

Petra turns quickly. 'Who are you?' she asks Zoe.

But Zoe looks at Mark. 'Are you OK?' she asks him.

'Yes,' says Mark, getting off the chair. He is pleased to see his sister. 'I saw the smoke. What did you do?'

Zoe smiles. 'I started a fire.'

Petra is moving across to her, but Zoe pushes over a chair before the woman gets to her. 'Run!' she shouts at Mark. Then she pulls the table in front of Petra.

Mark runs out of the house. Petra tries to stop him, but the boy is too quick for her. She catches Zoe as the girl starts to run to the door.

'Got you!' says Petra, catching Zoe's arm.

Zoe kicks the woman hard and pulls herself away. She runs out of the house, looking up at the sky and trying to see the helicopter.

Mark is looking up at the sky too. 'There it is!' he shouts. 'It's getting nearer!'

George, Harry and Andy don't see Zoe or Mark. They are watching the fire burning.

'Look at all that money,' says Andy.

Harry sees the black bags. 'Somebody has made a fire with the money!' he shouts.

'Half a million pounds,' says Harry. He wants to cry.

George is angry. He wants to kill somebody. But then he has something more important to think about.

'The helicopter is back!' he shouts at the other two. 'They can see us! *Run!*'

♦

The policeman and policewoman in the helicopter see the people running behind the farm buildings. They see a girl and a boy, and three men and a woman. The girl and boy are running to the stables. The men and the woman are running across the flooded fields, away from the farm house. They are looking up at the helicopter.

'What's happening down there?' says the policeman flying the helicopter.

'Something's wrong,' says the policewoman. 'Look! Three men and a woman! Perhaps it's the security van robbers.'

'Call for some help,' says the policeman flying the helicopter. 'Then let's go down and have a look.'

'OK,' says the policewoman. And she picks up the police radio and starts to talk into it.

♦

'They're getting away!' says Zoe, watching the robbers running through the water. She and Mark are standing outside the stables. They can see George and Petra running across one field, and Harry and Andy running across another. Above them, the police helicopter is coming down slowly. Zoe can see the people inside it.

'The police can't catch all four of the robbers,' says Mark. 'Two of them are going to get away. They're

The policeman and policewoman in the helicopter see the people running behind the farm buildings.

running through the trees.'

Zoe thinks for a minute, then she says, 'No, they're not going to get away!' And she runs into the stables and comes out with Topaz.

'What are you going to do?' asks Mark.

'Topaz and I are going after the two running through the trees,' says Zoe. 'Perhaps the helicopter can't get down there, but we can!'

Mark watches his sister jump on to the horse. Minutes later, she is following Harry and Andy across the field.

Harry sees Zoe and the horse coming after him.

'Look!' he shouts to Andy. Andy turns round to look – and runs into a tree! He falls into the water under the tree and doesn't move.

Harry tries to get away but Topaz soon catches him.

'Stop!' shouts Zoe.

Harry is afraid of the horse. He stops running and holds up his hands. 'OK, OK! I'm not running any more. You've got me. Don't let that horse get near me!'

'Help your friend to stand up and go back to the farm,' Zoe tells him. 'I'm going to follow you.'

Harry helps Andy to stand up and they go across the fields, back to the farm house. Zoe follows behind them on her horse.

Three police cars are coming fast down the small road next to the fields. The helicopter is flying over George and Petra. The two robbers have seen the police cars.

'We can't get away,' says Petra.

George stops running. He is very tired. 'I can't run any more,' he says.

After a minute, they put up their hands and start to walk over to the road and the police cars.

Harry sees Zoe and the horse coming after him. 'Look!' he shouts to Andy. Andy turns round to look . . .

*The policeman and policewoman are talking to Zoe and Mark.
'It was lucky I had money to burn!' laughs Zoe.*

'What happened to Harry and Andy?' George asks Petra. 'Did they get away?'

Petra looks across to the other field. She sees Harry helping Andy, followed by the girl on the horse. 'No,' she tells George, 'they didn't get away.'

◆

Fifteen minutes later, the helicopter is standing behind the barn. The policeman and policewoman from it are talking to Zoe and Mark in the farm house. The police cars have gone, taking the four robbers with them.

'That was clever, making a fire for us to see,' the policeman says to Zoe.

'It was lucky I had money to burn!' laughs Zoe.

EXERCISES

Vocabulary Work

Look back at the 'Dictionary Words' in this story. Do you know *all* the words?

1 Look at all the pictures. In which of the pictures can you see these things? Write the word and the number of the right page.

a a farm   f stables
b banknotes   g a lighter
c a fence   h blood
d a sign   i a helicopter
e a barn   j a ladder

Write short sentences about *where* the things are, or what the people in the pictures are doing with them.

2 Write sentences with the words in these groups.

a security van/shouts
b storm/blowing/flooded
c lighter/burned/banknotes

Comprehension

Chapters 1–2

1 Who said or thought these words?

a Nothing must go wrong.
b 'Do you think the wind blew that tree down, Frank?'
c 'I don't like storms.'
d 'Can't you go faster?'
e 'Half a million pounds! We're rich!'

Chapters 3–4

2 The Harpers' farm has these buildings in it:

THE FARM HOUSE   THE BARN   THE STABLES

Where do these things happen in these chapters? Write HOUSE BARN or STABLES to finish the sentences.

a There are three horses in the . . .

b Petra drives the car into the old . . . and the three men go over to the . .

c Mark is watching from the doors of the . . . He sees Harry come ou of the . . .

Chapters 5–6

3 Find the answers to these questions.

a Where did Harry lose his lighter?

b Why can't Zoe drive the red car?

c How may policemen are in the helicopter?

d What does Zoe use to make the fire?

Discussion

1 Mr and Mrs Harper didn't take Zoe and Mark to the hospital because of the storm and the dangerous roads. Was this the right thing to do?

2 Do you think Zoe was clever? Why? How?

3 Harry, George, Andy and Petra were not very good people.

a Did you like *any* of them? Who? Why?

b Were you sorry for any of them? Who? Why?

Writing

1 Look at the picture on page 23.

a Write three sentences about Andy's face, body and clothes.

b Write three sentences about George's face, body and clothes.

2 Finish the following sentences.

a The security van stopped because . . .

b Mr Harper went to hospital because . . .

c The robbers went to the farm because . . .

3 You are behind a tree and the robbery happens. You see it happen. Now write 100–150 words for the newspapers, telling the story.